INSTANT FUN FOR ALL KINDS OF GROUPS

FOR ALL

ASSOCIATION PRESS

INSTANT FUN

KINDS OF GROUPS

LORRELL COFFMAN BURNS

NEW YORK

793
BƆG

INSTANT FUN FOR ALL KINDS OF GROUPS

Copyright © 1964 by
National Board of Young Men's Christian Associations

Association Press   291 Broadway   New York, N.Y.   10007

Publisher's stock number: 1552
Library of Congress catalog card number: 64-18212

 2

PRINTED IN THE UNITED STATES OF AMERICA

Dedicated

to the Memory of My Parents

Joseph Warren and Mary Creola Coffman

Who Taught Us at Home from Childhood

the Real Joy of

Play and Laughter

Author's Preface

For many years we have been wondering why someone did not take a number of choice old games, songs, and stunts, and make them live and sparkle again. In keeping with the trend toward more quickies for small-group activities to large groups with minimum participation in entertainment, we have tried to make this a reality by bringing out *Instant Fun for All Kinds of Groups.*

In preparing this material we had in mind the many inexperienced hostesses and leaders who need games and material that can be easily and quickly understood and used. The descriptions may seem lengthy, but our experience for many years as a recreational director, and our having been behind the bookstore counter trying to help leaders find usable materials, has made us keenly aware of the need for full directions. That is why we have followed the pattern of presenting each game in four steps: Materials, Formation, Directions, Variations.

Pay special attention to the variations following most games. Be sure to read these each time. Develop your imagination, and soon you will have your own ideas for adapting game material. These are only suggestions; add your ideas, and you will be successful in directing your own new games. Many times the variations are better than the original game.

Most of the properties are very easy to get. It is a good idea to work up a group of games and keep a supply of properties in your recreation file, ready for instant use. For example, take the game "I'm the Guy." We have eight or ten variations ready to use for almost any occasion. It takes only a few minutes to step to the corner drugstore for a supply of wrapped candy for the game. We have used this game with groups of five to 100 and have never seen it fall on its face. The same thing is true with the simple little "Pass the Pencil Relay"—we have never yet had it fail to bring down the house.

The Cross-Reference Index has been set up by numbered games or stunts to help you find materials on certain subjects easily. Don't stop with only those suggested here— make your own index. The games are numbered so that they can be found much more quickly. No doubt we have failed to mention many other uses of these stunts and games, but you can adapt them to suit your needs. We hope you will have as much fun referring to this book as we have had in preparing it.

We are most grateful to the many, many friends who have allowed us to practice on them with all this material. It has been used on all ages and on groups of from five to 500 in size.

We have always been grateful to the many wonderful leaders in the field of recreation. We wish for every user great joy and fun in striving to make people laugh and to make them happy. A laughing group is a happy group.

We have tried to secure permission to use materials when we knew the source. We apologize if we have failed to give credit where credit is due.

Contents

Cross-Reference Index

GAMES WHICH are suitable for the following twelve occasions or circumstances are listed here by their numbers as they appear throughout the book.

Assemblies and Camp Activities: 1, 2, 3, 4, 6, 7, 8, 9, 10, 11, 13, 17, 20, 22, 23, 24, 26, 27, 28, 29, 30, 31, 33, 34, 35, 36, 38, 39, 40, 42, 43, 44, 45, 46, 47.

Banquets: 5, 25, 26, 32, 33, 37, 40, 41, 42, 46, 47.

Birthday Celebrations: 12, 15, 17, 18, 19, 20, 29, 30, 41.

Bridal and Baby Showers: 8, 12, 14, 17, 18, 20, 21, 28.

Church Fellowships (Young People and Adults): 1, 2, 3, 4, 6, 7, 8, 9, 10, 11, 13, 14, 15, 16, 17, 22, 24, 25, 26, 27, 28, 30, 31, 32, 33, 34, 35, 36, 37, 38, 39, 40, 42, 43, 44, 45, 46, 47.

Golden Age Entertainment: 1, 2, 5, 6, 8, 9, 11, 14, 15, 16, 17, 18, 19, 20, 21, 22, 23, 28, 30, 31, 39, 44, 45, 46, 47.

Halloween Time: 8, 9, 12, 15, 18, 20, 24, 27, 35, 43, 44.

Junior Boys and Girls: 1, 2, 5, 6, 7, 10, 30, 31, 33, 37, 41, 42, 43, 44, 45, 46, 47.

Luncheons: 3, 5, 11, 16, 17, 18, 19, 20, 21, 23, 25, 26, 28, 29, 30, 31, 32, 33, 35, 37, 39, 40, 41, 42, 43, 47.

Picnics: 1, 2, 3, 6, 7, 8, 9, 10, 23, 25, 27.

Seasonal Affairs: 4, 6, 9, 10, 12, 13, 14, 16, 17, 18, 25, 26, 27, 28, 30, 35, 36, 37, 38, 39.

Valentine Affairs: 4, 6, 12, 19, 21, 28, 32, 35, 36.

INSTANT

ACTION GAMES

Chapter 1

THESE GAMES are "instant" because they can be learned quickly at one trial by any group. They require minimum preparation by the leader, and the simple "props" can be made easily ahead of time. The following are only a few. Leaders should build up their own game file of such material.

1. The Blow-Out

Material:

List various automobile parts on a card.

Formation:

Players seated in a circle with an extra player standing as the Mechanic.

Directions:

The Mechanic, appointed by the leader, takes the list and walks around the circle, giving each player the name of some part of a car. Then he steps to the center and calls for various parts. Those people must come to the center and fall in line behind the Mechanic. He calls other parts as he marches around, forming an inner circle, not too close to the outside circle. At any unexpected moment the Mechanic calls BLOW-OUT. At that, the seated players must change chairs, taking any except the ones immediately next to them. The other players including the Mechanic dash for seats in this scramble. The one failing to get a seat becomes the new Mechanic. He receives the card list and starts the inner circle again.

Variations:

For an all-girl party use a Model and include in the list the articles of dress she will model. When the Model calls out PERFUME SPILLED, all scramble for a seat.

At a picnic the word GARLIC could be used with the names of picnic food for the list.

2. Peanuts

Materials:

A paper bag of unshelled peanuts for each leader.

Formation:

Informal—indoors or outdoors.

Directions:

Players number off by fours or sixes (or by twos if the group is small) to divide the group into teams. Each team takes the name of an animal and chooses a captain. When the teams are formed, all the players stand in a big circle while the game leader scatters peanuts inside the circle.

At a signal each player dashes to find a peanut, puts his toe lightly over it, and starts making the noise of his animal, barking, meowing, or whatever until his leader comes to pick up the peanut. Only the team leader can pick up a peanut. Team leader must listen sharply to hear the calls of his team. The team whose animal leader gets the largest number of peanuts in his sack is the winner.

Play the game at least twice so that each leader will get enough peanuts for all his animals. This is such a spirited game that most groups will want a number of repeats. Be prepared to sweep up shells whether used indoors or outdoors.

Variations:

For a small group use hazelnuts, pecans, or any nut or wrapped candy pieces suitable to the occasion. Have only two teams. Number off by twos—team No. 1 the Cats, team No. 2, the Dogs. All animals close eyes (no peeping) while leader places nuts about the room—or scatters them on the floor if space is large enough. If they are placed on the floor, follow the game as given above. If the nuts are on furniture in the room, the animal finding one must kneel before the nut and make his noise until the leader comes to pick it up. For older adults, change the kneeling to pointing at the nut with index finger.

It is fun to wrap the nuts or candy in blue paper for the Dogs and red for the Cats. Animals may call for their leader to pick up nut of his enemy. For example, a Cat will try to get all the red items he can, and the more blue ones his leader can steal from the Dogs, the better chance the Cats will have to win. The winner is the team that has the largest number of its own color. Again, only the *leader* can pick up any nut or candy.

3. Give Me a Clue

Materials:

Slips of paper prepared ahead of time, each with a sentence describing action to be performed by individuals. Have two sets exactly alike.

Formation:

Informal.

Description:

Distribute one set of slips to girls and one set to boys. Warn each player to keep his paper a secret. At the signal each girl starts acting out the instruction on her slip. Each boy moves about trying to identify the girl who is acting out the instruction on his paper. When he properly identifies the girl, she becomes his partner for the evening, the next game, or refreshments.

Some Action Lines

1. Hum softly "Let Me Call You Sweetheart."
2. Wear a big broad grin until recognized.
3. Hold hand at back of head as an Indian wears a feather in his headband.
4. Walk around, limping on left foot.
5. Slip away and stand in a corner with your face to to the wall.
6. Pretend to write a letter to your sweetheart.
7. Scold your boy friend, using a chair to represent him.
8. Hold a bottle for the baby in your arms.
9. Knit a pair of socks.
10. Sing up and down the scale, using ha, ha, ha.
11. Imitate a girl who sees a mouse.

12. Recite dramatically your favorite Mother Goose rhyme.
13. Count loudly as far as you can in one breath, repeating until caught.
14. Give every girl a kiss on the cheek.
15. Keep spelling your first name backwards rapidly and loud enough to be heard.
16. Pretend to spank a bad little boy.
17. Put on your mascara very carefully.
18. Moan with severe back pains.
19. Imitate a political campaign speaker.
20. Act out your first plane flight.

4. King and Queen

Material:

Make a crown ahead of time, to be awarded to the winner.

Formation:

Players are seated in a circle. The leader stands inside the circle in front of his chair.

Directions:

Chairs are numbered around the circle, beginning with the first chair to the left of leader. Players are given a second to remind themselves of their chair numbers.

The leader calls any number, say "Nine." Instantly, the person in the ninth chair must call some other number. If any player answers to the wrong chair number, or fails to call out promptly, or if a player should call his own number, which often happens, that player goes to the last or highest numbered chair in the circle, and all the others move up one seat. This gives each player a different number to remember because the numbers of the chairs remain the same throughout the game. It is more fun to call numbers near the head as often as possible, causing more players to move each time. Keep the game moving rapidly, so that the players have to stay very alert. At the close of the game, the person seated in chair No. 1 is crowned King or Queen.

Variations:

Use this game for a seasonal festival and crown a Queen. The leader will seat a girl in chair No. 1 to begin the game. Leader should see that a boy is in chair No. 2 and that the remainder of the chairs will be mixed seating. The girls will work together to try to unseat the

Queen while the boys will work together to keep her in the chair. If the girls do move her, the boy seated next to her will move up to become the King for the girls if they can keep him in the chair. If the boy has to go to the foot, then the person who next moves to chair No. 1 may be either a boy or girl. Announce that you are going to let them elect their King or Queen. Explain the details after all are seated. This will prevent all the girls or all the boys trying to be in the first group of chairs. The winner will be crowned as either King or Queen of the evening.

5. Bottle and Match Magic

Materials:

Quart milk bottles or any bottles with about a two-inch mouth. A large box of regular-size kitchen matches, and game tables.

Formation:

One bottle in center of each table. Assign five or even six persons to each table. Players may find seats without assignment.

Directions:

Give each person ten matches. At a signal, the first player at each table places a match across the top of the bottle. Play then moves to the right, each player placing a match in turn, being careful not to knock other matches off. If a player knocks off a match or matches, he has to add them to his stock. First player to exhaust his supply of matches is declared winner.

After each table has a winner, each winner is given ten more matches to add to his supply. Each builds on the matches stacked on the bottle on his table to see who can build the highest stack. The winner is crowned King or Queen.

Variations:

Give each person a handful of matches. Allow each person a half-minute to see how many matches he can place on the bottle. He does not have to pick up the ones that fall.

6. Fourth of July Firecrackers

Materials:

Paper bags, medium-small size.

Formation:

Teams in parallel lines, each with a captain, and not more than 20 players per team.

Directions:

When teams are in line, the captains give a new, folded paper bag to each player, and tell him to place his folded bag under his right foot. When the leader gives the signal, the last player in each line picks up his bag, blows it up, and explodes it on the back of the person in front of him. That person then grabs his bag and performs the same action on the player in front of him. When this has been repeated down the line and it is the captain's turn, he inflates the bag, runs to the foot of the line, and explodes it on the back of the last player. The team whose captain does this first is declared winner. The contest will be close, so provide enough bags for another round, or the best two out of three. The captains move to the foot of the line and the player left at the head of the line becomes the new captain.

Variations:

For adults, use small candy bags, and let a team of men compete with a team of women. This gives the men an opportunity to be as rough as they like when breaking the bags on their buddies' backs.

7. Family Ford Relay

Materials:

Prepare a typed list of various parts of the Ford car. List and number the parts that can be dramatized or imitated.

Formation:

Two parallel lines with a captain for each line. Number the players, starting with the captain as No. 1. Set a goal line.

Directions:

Assign the same part of the Ford to each player with the same number in each line. For example, No. 1 is the bad steering gear and must walk zigzag to the goal and return; upon his return he touches off the second person. No. 2 is a flat tire, limping to the goal and back, and touching off the third person. No. 3 is water in the gas, taking two steps forward and one step back (sputtering). No. 4 travels in reverse gear, walking backwards. No. 5 is a dead battery and cannot go at all. No. 6 pushes No. 5 to the goal and back.

Think of other parts, or start over with No. 1 until everyone in the line has been to the goal and back. The first Ford to finish the relay is declared winner.

Variations:

Develop parts using other methods of transportation—trains, planes, ships, trucks, and so on.

8. Pass the Pencil Relay

Materials:

A long, slim pencil, or a long stick of licorice wrapped in cellophane for each team. Adapt for special holidays, using a candy cane for Christmas, striped Halloween candy, and the like.

Formation:

Select captains and form two teams of equal number, in parallel lines.

Directions:

Players in each team face their captain. The object is to see which team receiving the pencil from the leader and his helper can pass it down the line and back again first. This is more difficult than it sounds. The captain holds the pencil at one end, *between his top lip and nose,* and passes it to his first player just back of him. This player with his hands crossed back of himself, receives the pencil with his lip and nose in the same manner. Each player keeps hands folded behind him and cannot use them except to pick up pencil when it is dropped. After the captain passes the pencil successfully to the first player, he can follow along the line encouraging his team members. The only help he can give is to balance the pencil. If a player cannot pucker his lips enough to hold the pencil, the captain must work with him to help him balance it long enough to pass it back to the next in line. If he has to use his hands, he must step to the foot of the line and the captain may take his place. This exchange must be approved by the leader of the game or his helper. Play this game through once for practice. The second time it will move faster and with much more enthusiasm.

Variations:

For adults, place men in one line and women in the other. Change the color of the pencil or candy to fit any special season or holiday.

9. Apple Eaters

Materials:

Apples, paring knives, the number depending on size of party.

Formation:

Divide group into teams of four by counting off by fours.

Directions:

Each line of four stands one behind the other facing the goal. Place an apple and a knife on a chair or a table about twenty feet from each line. Player No. 1 in each line stands toeing the starting line. At a signal, the first player on each team runs to the goal and peels the apple, keeping the peeling all in one piece, if possible. If the peeling is unbroken, the team gets an extra ten points. The second player is touched off by player No. 1. Rushing to the goal, he quarters the apple; player No. 3 removes the core; No. 4 eats the apple and returns to his place in the line. The first team to finish wins 20 points, plus 10 if peeling is not broken. If peeling is broken, the team gets minus 10 points.

For the second round, player No. 1 goes to the foot, and player No. 2 takes his place. Continue until all four players on each team have eaten an apple. The team with the highest number of points wins. Scorekeepers and judges stay at goal lines to see that each player operates correctly.

Variations:

Instead of apples, provide crackers and peanut butter. The first player spreads a tablespoonful of peanut butter on the cracker and runs back to the second player. Player No. 2 eats the cracker, then dashes back to the third player, who spreads peanut butter on another cracker. Player No. 4 eats the second cracker.

For a summer garden party, have boiled ears of corn. The first player applies the butter, the second, salt; the third, pepper; player No. 4 eats the corn, leaving only the cob. Continue until all four players in each line have eaten an ear of corn.

10. Bird Rhythm

Materials:
Each line of Bird Alphabet is typed and clipped, so that each player gets a copy of one line. Pins.

Formation:
Informal—icebreaker game.

Directions:
As each guest arrives, helpers assist leader in pinning a typed line on left shoulder. Be sure the lists are well mixed. If any lines are left over, ask some players to take two lines instead of one. As soon as all lines are pinned, the leader announces that the alphabet has been used to list twenty-six birds each in a two-line rhyme. Players must complete the bird couplet by matching the last word in each line. Allow about fifteen minutes or less, depending on size of crowd and rapidity of action.

As each bird finds his rhyme line, he reports to the leader and he and his partner get into alphabetical order to build the Bird Rhyme alphabet. When all are in line, the leader signals to A and each player in turn reads his line dramatically.

Bird Rhythm Alphabet List

A is for Acadian Flycatcher, you see
   He builds his home far up in a tree.

B is for Bluebird, all dressed in his best;
   He has been called the bird of happiness.

C is for Crow, you may shoot, says the law,
   But he only replies with his lusty "Caw, Caw."

D is for Dove, you know by her call;
   Her song is most plaintive when heard in the fall.

E is for Eagle, symbol of our nation;
   He sits on our flagpole with great admiration.

F stands for a bird that is known as the Flicker,
   And in pecking on trees no bird could be quicker.

G is for Geese, as they go speeding by,
   They "honk" to each other way up in the sky.

H is for Horned Lark, he builds on the ground,
   So early in the springtime that snow is around.

I is for Indigo Bunting so blue
   He looks like a bit of the sky fallen through.

J is for Jay Bird, you must know one kind—
   Canada, Florida, Blue you will find.

K is for Kingfisher, swooping down with a swish.
   He comes up carrying a wriggling fish.

L is for Love Bird, the pet of the wood.
   Although she's a favorite, she's not very good.

M is for Meadow Lark, and out in the West
   He sings his sweet songs at his very best.

N is for the Nuthatch, a good friend to man.
   He clears all the bugs and worms off his land.

O is for Oriole, black and yellow.
   His song in the orchard is soft and mellow.

P is for Parrot, the clown among birds;
   When he stays around people, he learns to say
      words.

Q is for Quail, so cunning and wise.
   She'll pretend to be wounded, her home to disguise.

R is for Red Wing, the black bird you see,
   Singing his early spring song: "O-Ka-Lee."

S is for Swallow, I'm sure you agree,
   No bird is so lovely and graceful as he.

T is for Towhee, sometimes called woods robin.
   In piles of dry leaves you'll see him a-bobbin'.

U is for Uhu, German for owl.
They sleep through the day, and at night they do
     prowl.
V stands for Vireo; he has a red eye.
All summer long you can hear his cry.
W is for Wrens and the songs that they sing
Make all the dooryards with happiness ring.
X is for all the birds I don't know.
If they were all together, they'd make a great show.
Y is for the Yellowhammer, I just now recall,
He's kin to the Flicker—now really, that's all.
Z is for the Zoo where strange birds are collected.
They have the best care while they are protected.

Variations:

When used with children, assign a "letter" to each
to memorize. Encourage each child to learn the song
of his bird and to imitate it after he has recited his lines.

Adults and young people can give the song imitations for the audience to guess, before giving the lines.
This game is best used in a program built around birds,
or other nature theme.

(Adapted with the permission of Miss Lucille Stevenson, Oklahoma City)

Chapter 2

INSTANT
WRITE-IN
GAMES

11. Horse Sense

Materials:

"Suggested List" of names or objects mimeographed or typed, as given below *without* the answers. Pencils.

Formation:

Informal seating.

Directions:

Leader hands out the mimeographed lists and pencils. At the signal, each player unfolds his sheet and starts underlining the correct answer to each question. Allow about 15 minutes if a long list is used. Work out a scoring system, such as 0-5, poor; 6-12, average; 13-20, superior; 21-up, very superior.

Suggested List

1. The name of Cheshire suggests which sound? Ba-a, cackle, moo, meow. (meow)
2. Mint jelly should indirectly suggest which one of these storybook characters? Little Bo-Peep, Three Little Pigs, Red Riding Hood, Little Red Hen. (Little Bo-Peep)
3. The mother of a filly would make which sound? Neigh, bray, bleat, low. (neigh)
4. The numbers 9x12 are most suggestive of which name? Dresden, Chippendale, Axminster, Florsheim. (Axminster)
5. Billy the Kid suggests which typical sound? Beep, ding dong, bzz, bang bang. (bang bang)
6. Wilbur Wright suggests which item? Weather vane, brake shoe, spark plug, wind shock. (wind shock)
7. A cotter pin is most suggestive of which type of worker? Carpenter, machinist, plumber, roofer. (machinist)

8. The father of a mule makes which characteristic sound? Whinny, oink, heehaw, moo. (heehaw)

9. In its childhood, a gelding was called? Shoat, foal, kitten, cub. (foal)

10. In its original state, an Axminster made which typical sound? Moo, oink, cackle, ba-a. (ba-a)

11. One ton of which one of the following will occupy the most space? Coke, anthracite, lead. (coke, for it's the lightest)

12. Which one of these produces the quickest attack of itching after contact? Poison sumac, poison ivy, nettles, poison oak. (nettles)

13. Which one of these terms suggests the police? Cast, roster, roll, line-up. (line-up)

14. A "dandy roller" is used by which one of these workers? Candy maker, pie maker, paper maker. (paper maker for watermark)

15. Which one of these holds the most gallons? Barrel, nail keg, hogshead, demijohn. (hogshead, 63 gallons)

16. The land that "flowed with milk and honey" should suggest which city? Rome, Babylon, Jericho, Tarsus. (Jericho)

17. The log cabin was introduced to America by which nationality? English, German, Swedes, Spanish. (Swedes)

18. Five animals contribute meat items to our dinner. Match the animals with the meats.

Doe	Mutton chops
Sow	Giblets
Capon	Ham
Steer	Venison
Ewe	T-bone steak

(doe-venison, sow-ham, capon-giblets, steer-steak, ewe-mutton)

19. A person who travels by "shank's mare" goes by which method? Automobile, airplane, boat, afoot. (afoot)

20. A drover would suggest which one of these? Black Beauty, Bo-Peep, Cow-that-jumped-over-the-moon, Humpty Dumpty. (cow)

21. Humpty-Dumpty belonged to which one of these groups? Clutch, herd, swarm, drove. (Clutch of eggs)

22. A poult should indirectly suggest which one of these sports? Tennis, bowling, baseball, football. (bowling, turkey)

23. In slang terms, a sawbuck refers to which paper bill in our currency? $2, $5, $10, $20. ($10)

24. The mother of a maverick would make which type of sound? Neigh, bray, bleat, low. (low)

25. Three of the following are virus diseases—which one is not? Mumps, chickenpox, smallpox, diphtheria. (diphtheria)

26. A mortar and pestle suggest which of the following workers? Carpenter, bricklayer, plumber, druggist. (druggist)

27. Five tools or instruments are normally used in the daily work of the five men indicated in the righthand column. Match them.

Skewer	Farmer
Cotter Pin	Carpenter
Claw hammer	Machinist
Combine	Plumber
Wrench	Chef

(Skewer-Chef, Cotter pin-Machinist, Claw hammer-Carpenter, Combine-Farmer, Wrench-Plumber)

Variation:

Instead of a mimeographed list given to players, the leader may call out four words. Three words belong in the same classification, one does not. Players are given ten seconds to call out the word that does not belong in the group. Practice on the first four words so all will understand. (Add other sets of words to fit into theme of affair.)

Suggested List

1. Hoover, Coolidge, Harding, Pershing. (General Pershing does not belong in the group of U. S. Presidents)
2. Orchestra, drum, horn, violin. (Orchestra)
3. Rose, squash, pansy, violet. (squash)
4. Perch, salmon, snake, bass. (snake)
5. Wagon, spade, hoe, rake. (wagon)
6. Ford, Chevrolet, sedan, Dodge. (sedan)
7. Violet, blue, bright, orange. (bright)
8. Shoes, slippers, dress, overshoes. (dress)
9. Wet, cold, rainy, damp. (cold)
10. Dark, shadowy, cloudy, sunshine. (sunshine)
11. Lawyer, doctor, chemist, clerk. (clerk)
12. Piano, notes, rests, clef. (piano)
13. Minister, superintendent, pastor, preacher. (superintendent)
14. Cellophane, linen, voile, crêpe. (cellophane)
15. Canal, street, stream, brook. (street)

12. Intelligence Test

Materials:

Copy of test *without* the letters written above the lines, for each guest. Pencils.

Formation:

Informal seating.

Directions:

This variation of the game can be used to announce the distribution of gifts at a Christmas party. Give a pencil and a copy of the test to guests with instructions not to start until the signal is given. The guests can read the questions, or the leader can read them aloud. As each guest finishes the test, he comes to stand by the leader. When all have finished, the leader gives a signal for all to read in unison. Then Santa comes in to distribute the gifts.

An Intelligence Test

Note: With a calm mind and hand, write the proper letters over the proper numbers.

(S)	(A)	(N)
1	2	3
(T)	(A)	(C)
4	5	6
(L)	(A)	(U)
7	8	9
(S)	(I)	(S)
10	11	12
(C)	(O)	(M)
13	14	15

(I)	(N)	(G)
16	17	18

1. If you ever saw a cow jump over the moon, write "no" in spaces 1, 10, 12. If not, write "S" in these spaces.
2. If "Z" comes before "H" in the alphabet, write "Z" in spaces 3 and 17. If it comes after "H," write "N."
3. If 31,467 is more than a dozen, write "A" in spaces 2, 5, and 8.
4. If you like candy more than mosquitoes, write "T" in space 4. If not, better consult an alienist at once.
5. Close one eye and without counting on your fingers, write the third letter in the alphabet in spaces 6 and 13.
6. If Shakespeare wrote "Twinkle, twinkle little star" put "O" in space 7, otherwise write "L."
7. If white and black are opposite, write "U" in space 9, "I" in space 11, and "G" in space 18. If some other color, write nothing.
8. If ten quarts make one pint, draw an elephant in space 14 and 16. Otherwise write "O" in space 14 and "I" in space 16.
9. If summer is warmer than winter, put an "M" in space 15; if not, put "L" in that space.
10. If you think this is foolish, all well and good, but now read what you have written. Something is going to happen!

Variations:

Use this game to announce refreshments. The words "Refreshments Served" fit the 18 blanks. Just change the letters in the instructions. For a birthday, "Happy Birthday Deary" will fit the 18 blanks. Use your imagination to make the test longer or shorter for "April Fool," and other occasions.

13. Burlesque (do not announce the name of this game until the end)

Materials:

Pencils and slips of paper.

Formation:

Informal seating.

Directions:

Ask each player to write his name, including nickname, home address and where he works, or occupation, on the slip of paper. Have him fold three or four times to conceal the information completely. Collect papers in a box. Pass the box of shuffled names around for each guest to draw one slip. Caution each to keep the information on his slip a secret. Each player gets two minutes to decide how he will act out the name he has drawn. Allow guests to use any properties that are needed and accessible. The best actor can be declared the winner, or the other players can try to guess what person is being imitated.

Variations:

At a patriotic party, use a list of national figures instead of the names of those players present. Allow two minutes to work up actions to dramatize the character. For a variety show, make up a list of TV and movie stars, and assign these to each guest to make sure the best imitations may be given, such as singing, dancing, Western movie scenes.

14. Eggs-amination Questions

Materials:

A hard-boiled egg for each player. It can be colored a pastel shade or just natural. Pencils or ball-point pens.

Formation:

Group is seated in a circle or around a table.

Directions:

Leader passes eggs and pencils to players. Each is asked to print his two initials plainly on the large end of the egg. Then the eggs are passed clockwise around until the leader has counted off to No. 10. On the count of ten, each player holds the egg in his hand. The leader reads a question and each player has to write the answer to that question in two words, using the initial on his egg. Example: Initial "O.B." and to the question "What is your favorite saying?" he might write "Oh, bologna!" Allow about a minute for players to write the two-word answer to each question. Players number each answer.

When the last question has been answered, the eggs are passed again clockwise while the leader counts to ten. Then each person in consecutive order stands, gives the name of the person whose initials are on his egg and then gives the answers written on the egg. The leader reads the questions back to make the answers sound funnier, or they may be written out on a poster to display, or on a chalkboard, or perhaps mimeographed so that each player may have a copy. At the close of eggs-amination, each players gets his own initialed egg to keep.

Questions

1. What does "IT" (meaning person whose initials are on egg) look like?
2. What does "IT" love?
3. What is "ITS" favorite occupation?
4. What is "ITS" favorite recreation?
5. What is "ITS" one good quality?

(Used by permission of T. S. Denison and Co.)

15. Shadow the Following Persons

Materials:

Pencils, and mimeographed lists of questions given below.

Formation:

An informal mixer.

Directions:

When most of the guests have arrived, distribute the sheets and pencils. Each guest begins filling in the blanks on his sheet. This is a good mixer, so allow some fifteen minutes for all to seek information. At a signal, ask the group to be seated. Ask someone to volunteer to read his answers. The leader reads the question and the player calls the name of the person. That person then comes to the center. A guest may challenge the name of the person if he feels the information about the guest is incorrect. If the player has been incorrect, the one who challenged takes his place. If he is correct, he continues reading. This group called to the front then becomes the honor group—at a break time in the entertainment they are to present a stunt. The leader should be prepared with several ideas to be sure of a good stunt. This mixer is especially good for a large banquet group before being seated at the table.

Questions

1. Give the full name of a person wearing a bow tie

_____

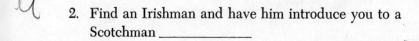

2. Find an Irishman and have him introduce you to a Scotchman _____

3. Find a woman with long hair and have her introduce you to a girl with blonde hair. Write both names here _____

4. If you have a brother, meet some other person's brother and have him introduce you to someone's sister. Name _____

5. Ask someone born West of the Rockies to introduce you to someone born East of the Rockies. Write both names here _____

6. Find a person whose surname begins with B, E, F, M or T. Ask him to introduce you to someone whose name begins with S, T, R, A or H. Write both names here _____

7. If you are a man and like onions, ask every woman you meet if she likes men who eat onions. When you find one that does, write her name here

   _____

8. If you do not prefer blondes, ask the first blonde (men ask women and women ask men) you meet to introduce you to a brunette. Write the brunette's name here _____

9. If you are a woman and like liver and onions, find a man who likes them also, and write his name here _____

10. Meet any red-haired person present and write name here _____

11. Get the name and height of the tallest man present _____ The shortest woman present

    _____

12. Ask a woman with an "up-sweep" hair-do to introduce you to a brown-eyed gentleman. Write both names here _____

Variations:

For a married, adult group, adjust questions to suit the situation, such as, married the longest, smallest number of children, largest number of children, and so on. For retired groups, ask: largest number of grandchildren, man with least amount of hair, best checker player, non-coffee drinker, most recent birthday, and the like.

16. Biblical Alphabet

Materials:

Ditto sheets of questions listed below, not including answers; pencils.

Formation:

Informal seating.

Directions:

Folded sheet and pencil is given to each player. Do not look at paper until signal is given. Five minutes is allowed to fill in the blanks with a noun from the Bible in alphabetical order. Player filling in largest number of blanks is winner. Award him according to the nature of your party.

Biblical Alphabet List

A. The first man _____ (Adam)

B. Joseph's youngest brother _____ (Benjamin)

C. Where Jesus performed his first miracle _____ (Cana)

D. A woman judge of Israel _____ (Deborah)

E. Adam's wife _____ (Eve)

F. Who trembled before Paul? _____ (Felix)

G. The Garden where Jesus prayed _____ (Gethsemane)

H. One of Noah's sons _____ (Ham)

I. Abraham's son _____ (Isaac)

J. His name was changed to Israel _____ (Jacob)

K. The father of Saul _____ (Kish)

L. A companion of Paul _____ (Luke)

M. The writer of the second Gospel _____ (Mark)

N. The builder of the ark _____ (Noah)

O. Ruth's sister _____ (Orpha)
P. The Apostle to the Gentiles _____ (Paul)
Q. A man that Paul called brother _____ (Quartus)
R. The wife of Isaac _____ (Rebekah)
S. The first king of Israel _____ (Saul)
T. A doubting disciple _____ (Thomas)
U. Bathsheba's first husband _____ (Uriah)
V. A beautiful queen _____ (Vashti)
W. The Magi who paid homage to the newborn King _____ (wise-men)
X. A short way to spell Christmas _____ (Xmas)
Y. What the oxen of the Bible wore _____ (Yoke)
Z. The father of James and John _____ (Zebedee)

Variations:

Leader may read the list and allow guests to call out the name needed for the blank. First person to call out is given a piece of candy. Arrange for chalkboard and first person to reach board writes the name. If he misspells name, second person is given a chance. Be sure there is no prompting.

17. Know Your Slogans U.S.A.

Materials:

Prepare slogans ahead of time on chalkboard or flip chart in two- or three-inch letters. Cover with newspaper strips. List answers on a card for leader's use only. Paper and pencils for player.

Formation:

Informal seating.

Directions:

Give each player a pencil and sheet of paper. Announce that at the signal everyone must write the name of the product the slogan advertises. Then pull one strip of newspaper off to reveal the slogan and continue until they all have been revealed. Award the winner with a sample of some product advertised.

Suggested Slogans

1. "But, we can't brush after every meal." (Gleem)
2. "It likes you and you like it." (7-Up)
3. "Where do you get all that energy?" From (Nestle's Quik-Milk)
4. "I'm Prudence Potts, the Pan Inspector." (Brillo Pads)
5. "You can always tell a _____ girl by the shine on her hair." (Halo)
6. "Be sure with _____." (Pure Oil Co.)
7. "Frosty, Man, Frosty." (Pepsi Cola)
8. "More people the world over stop at the _____." (Esso Sign)
9. "You'll be glad you got together." (National Life Ins.)
10. "Refresh with a pitcher of pleasure." (Lipton Tea)

11. "We sell the best and serve the rest." (Westinghouse)
12. "Promise her anything but give her _____." (Arpege)
13. "Baked while you sleep." (Tasty Bread)
14. "The most excitingly different cakes." (Duncan Hines)

Variations:

Cut samples of advertising and paste on sheets of paper, asking guests to write-in the slogan. Prepare enough for each to have two or three sheets. If used for a bridal or baby shower, use ads depicting appropriate articles. For a TV party use program titles and names of characters in shows. For Golden Age groups, use ads from daytime TV shows. Keep ads up to date. They change frequently.

18. What's Your Sign?

Materials:

Pencils and paper, with zodiac dates, as given below. (Also twelve small boxes for use under *Variations*.)

Formation:

Informal.

Directions:

Give each player a copy of the list "The Twelve Signs" and a pencil, and tell him to fill in each date with the name of someone present who was born under that sign. Allow ample time, then signal to stop. Select at random a sheet completed. Each one listed on that sheet becomes the leader of a zodiac group. For example, John Doe (Pisces) is leader for all present whose birthday is under the sign of the Fish. Players gather around their leaders. Each group must plan and put on some form of entertainment depicting that zodiac sign. After each performance, the leader can read the horoscope of that sign aloud.

The Twelve Signs

1. Scorpion (Scorpius, October 24-November 22)
   (name) _____
2. Fish (Pisces, February 19-March 20)
   (name) _____
3. Virgin (Virgo, August 24-September 23)
   (name) _____
4. Balance (Libra, September 24-October 25)
   (name) _____
5. Twins (Gemini, May 21-June 21)
   (name) _____

6. Archer (Sagittarius, November 23-December 21)
   (name) _____

7. Ram (Aries, March 21-April 19)
   (name) _____

8. Crab (Cancer, June 22-July 22)
   (name) _____

9. Water Bearer (Aquarius, January 20-February 18)
   (name) _____

10. Bull (Taurus, April 20-May 20)
    (name) _____

11. Goat (Capricorn, December 22-January 19)
    (name) _____

12. Lion (Leo, July 28-August 23)
    (name) _____

Variations:

Use for a birthday party or Hallowe'en party by having a gypsy fortuneteller seated at a table giving the fortune of each one according to his zodiac sign. These may be mimeographed and cut in strips placed in the twelve boxes to be sure each gets his proper fortune.

For a smaller dinner party, secure the birth date of each guest in advance. Type out the fortune of each, and attach it to one end of a narrow ribbon. Place the fortune end of ribbon in bowl in center of table, with ribbon extending to each plate, and fastened to a place card. Between dinner and dessert, the hostess can begin by reading her own fortune pulled from the center bowl. Each guest in turn then reads her fortune aloud.

19. Let's Write a Book

Materials:

Paper, pencils, and duplicate copies of story ("The Book Completed," below), one for each player.

Formation:

Seated informally.

Directions:

Distribute the paper and pencils, and announce, "The first step in writing a book is to set up an outline. Begin by numbering lines on your paper, from one to twenty-three." When everyone has finished, the leader reads out, one at a time, the "Book Outline Questions" given below, slowly enough for each player to write his answers on his numbered list. When this is finished, give each player a copy of the story on which to fill in the answers from his numbered list. If crowd is not too large, let each read his story, asking the person whose name is signed to stand up while his "book" is being read.

Book Outline Questions

Read Slowly

1. Write the name of a person present.
2. A year
3. Town
4. College
5. Yes or No
6. A number
7. Vocation *(Occupation - example: "Carpenter")*
8. An amount of money
9. Another amount of money
10. The word BIG or LITTLE
11. A number
12. A color

13. A habit
14. Individual in one's family, as "Sister"
15. Vegetable
16. Flower
17. Number
18. Animal
19. An activity *(Jump-walk)*
20. Sum of money
21. Name of person of opposite sex from the name on line one
22. Name something you like to do. *(Swim, Drive, Golf)*
23. Your name

Pass Your Paper to the Person on your Right)

The Book Completed

"A famous person among us whose name is (1) _Basie's_ was born in (2) _1932_ in the town of (3) _Vermont'll_. This famous person was educated at (4) _R.S.U._. He (or she) is married and when asked if happy, answered (5) _no_. He has (6) _25_ children and is a well-known (7) _hort_, earning (8) _25_ a year and spending (9) _25,000_ a year. He is a very (10) _little_ man wearing size (11) _43_ shoes and has (12) _green_ hair. He has a bad habit of (13) _biting_ which is due to his admiration of his (14) _mother_. He is a great gardener raising (15) _cauliflower_ (s) and (16) _tulips_ (s) which he will undoubtedly continue to grow and exhibit at garden shows until he is (17) _84_ years old. He loves pets, especially (18) _dogs_ and has been known to (19) _prostitute_ for their benefit. He has already bequeathed his (20) _$49_ to (21) _Van_ because he likes to (22) _sew_. Thus ends the story of (1) _____ and (21) _____ who lived happily ever after because I, (23) _Cheryl_, lie not."

20. The Family Secret

Materials:

Pencil and paper for each guest.

Formation:

Informal seating in circle or at a table. (luncheon)

Directions:

Make a brisk talk, about two minutes, on relatives, be they brothers, sisters, grandparents, or kissin' cousins. Example: "Friends, if you have as many relatives as I do, you may be embarrassed. But, I'm really curious about your relatives. I just wonder if you know how many you do have. If you're not too sure, I can help you find out—that is, if you'll do a little figuring. As I call out the instructions, write each correct answer under the one before, in a vertical column." Leader then asks each player to give him only the last figure. Leader can tell player, then, the exact number of brothers, sisters, and grandparents he has.

Chart

Write the number of your brothers	2
Multiply by two	4
Add three	7
Multiply by five	35
Add number of your sisters	37
Multiply by 10	370
Add number of living grandparents	372
Subtract 150	222

The first figure from left (in last number listed) tells the number of brothers, second is the number of sisters, and third the grandparents. Note: it will work the same should deceased family members be counted, but leader may announce that only those living are to be used.

21. You Name It!

Materials:

A sheet of paper and a pencil for each player. Paper can be blocked off into squares ahead of time, or players can make their own charts.

Formation:

Informal.

Directions:

Instruct each player to write a given key word in big letters across the top, and to "box" the letters by drawing vertical lines between them. Leave enough space between lines to hold a word. On the far, lefthand side of the paper, each player must write certain "categories" given by the leader. These categories may be such things as flowers, birds, rivers, cities, girls' names. A very simple chart might look like this:

	G	I	R	L
City	Genoa			
Vegetable				
Color				

At a signal, each player fills in the blank spaces with any name beginning with the right letter, and in the right category. *Genoa,* for example, might be used in the first square as a *city* beginning with g.

At another signal, players put away their pencils, and take turns reading across the chart. A word not used by anyone else scores 4 points, and all other words score 1. Player with highest scores wins.

Variations:

Make the top word suitable to the occasion: a girl's name if it is a birthday party for her, *witch* or *ghost* for Halloween; *flag* or *states* for patriotic occasion; *carol* or *gift* for Christmas, and the like.

This is an old, favorite game, useful because it is easily adapted to different age groups as well as to different occasions. It can be made simple or difficult, to suit the type of group.

22. Modern Questions with Biblical Answers

Materials:

Pencils and typed list of questions for each guest. Use only with groups that will not be offended by this type of game.

Formation:

Informal seating.

Directions:

Give each player a folded sheet of questions and a pencil. At a signal, the lists are opened and players given eight or ten minutes to fill in the blanks. Each player then signs his name and passes his paper to some other player to correct. To grade the papers allow five points for each correct answer. Leader may read the correct answers or select two players to read the questions alternately. The group will call out the answers.

Suggested Questions

1. Who crossed a sea without a boat? *(Children of Israel)*

2. Who was the first to travel in a submarine? *(Jonah)*

3. Who was the first circus man? *(Noah)*

4. Who took the first trip by air? *(Elijah)*

5. Who walked back from a boat ride? *(Peter)*

6. Name the first bird killed with a slingshot? *(Goliath)*

7. Who was the first lion tamer? *(Daniel)*

8. Who brought in the first gusher? *(Moses)*

9. Who was the first fortuneteller mentioned? *(Witch of Endor)*

10. What light failed Moses? *(Israelite)*

11. What was the longest day since the beginning of time? *(When Joshua commanded the sun to stand still)*

12. On which side of the boat were the fishermen told to cast their nets? *(On the other side)*

13. When was currency first mentioned in the Bible? *(When the dove brought the green back to the Ark.)*

14. Why did Noah send the dove? *(Because she had a bill)*

15. What proof have we that Lot's wife was not slender? *(She looked 'round)*

16. Why was Caesar restless? *(Because he was a Roman)* (a-roamin')

17. What reason do we have to believe that Eve had a bad disposition? *(Because she raised Cain)*

18. How long did Cain hate his brother? *(As long as he was Abel.)*

19. Why do we think of Job as a successful doctor? *(Because he had lots of patience)*

20. What was the most expensive haircut? *(Samson's)*

Variations:

Type individual questions and answers on separate slips of paper. Distribute both among the group. Player holding question No. 1 will stand and read the question.

The person who thinks he has the answer will stand and read it. If incorrect, the reader again asks the question, seeking the right answer. If the answer is correct they become partners for the next game. Continue until all are matched. Work out other sets of questions. These have been selected at random.

Used by permission of Mrs. Ed Stanley)

Chapter 3

INSTANT

BRAIN TEASERS

GAMES LIKE THESE are often seen on television or heard on radio. They are the "magic" games of camp, the do-as-I-do games of pantomime, the quizzes, and the games that require quick wits and fast responses. Here are only a few. Collect and add others. They make excellent icebreakers.

23. I'm the Guy

Materials:

Prepare a list of questions ahead of time. Use those listed here, adding local names for color. Provide plenty of candy kisses or wrapped candy to match the season or theme of occasion.

Formation:

Seat guests so that everyone can see the leader.

Directions:

The leader faces the group, and reads or asks the questions. A helper stands nearby, holding container of candy. As a question is asked, anyone who knows the answer jumps to his feet and shouts it out. If it is simpler, ask the player to raise his hand as he calls the answer. Leader and helper decide who was first to answer, and helper tosses him a piece of candy. In case of a tie both players get candy. If there are one or two who are especially alert and get most of the answers, try to spread the questions around. The leader may direct a question to a particular section of the room, or a special group, such as men only, or all players with blue eyes, or other improvised qualifications.

I'm the Guy

(Use this first question as an example to explain the game.)

— I'm the guy who freed the slaves. (Abraham Lincoln)
— I'm the guy who threw silver dollars across the Rappahannock. (George Washington)
— I'm the gal who wrote *Gone with the Wind*. (Margaret Mitchell)
— I'm the guy who established "Little America." (Admiral Byrd)

I'm the guy who invented the cotton gin. (Eli Whitney)

I'm the gal who charmed a king from his throne. (Wally Simpson)

I'm the guy who wrote the Declaration of Independence. (Thomas Jefferson)

I'm the gal who came between Caesar and Anthony. (Cleopatra)

I'm the guy who invented wireless telegraphy. (Marconi)

I'm the gal who is famous for my hatchet. (Carry A. Nation)

I'm the guy who invented the steamboat. (Robert Fulton)

I'm the guy who was the brother of Moses. (Aaron)

I'm the guy who wrote "Snowbound." (John G. Whittier)

I'm the gal who married Philip Mountbatten. (Princess Elizabeth)

I'm the guy who invented incandescent lights. (Thomas Edison)

I'm the guy who made love to Juliet. (Romeo)

I'm the guy who crossed the Alps into Italy. (Hannibal)

I'm the gal who ate the apple. (Eve)

I'm the guy who is "a bad-whitta-boy." (Red Skelton)

I'm the guy who said "Ah, Josephine, my Josephine." (Napoleon)

I'm the guy who was cast into the den of lions. (Daniel)

I'm the guy who had 1000 wives. (Solomon)

I'm the guy who discovered the Mississippi. (DeSoto)

I'm the gal who was loved by John Alden. (Priscilla)

I'm the first American to orbit the earth. (John Glenn)

I'm the guy who wrote the oratorio "The Messiah." (Handel)

I'm the king of England who had seven different wives. (Henry VIII)

I'm the guy famous for my fables. (Aesop)

I'm the gal who wrote *Little Women*. (Louisa M. Alcott)

I'm the guy who said "Go West, Young Man, Go West." (Horace Greeley)

I'm the gal who loves Popeye. (Olive Oil)

I'm the guy who was the first foreign missionary. (Apostle Paul)

I'm the guy who had a coat of many colors. (Joseph)

I'm the gal who saved the life of Captain John Smith. (Pocahontas)

I'm the guy who discovered the Pacific. (Balboa)

I'm the gal who was the first woman barber. (Delilah)

I'm the animal who has a "little red nose." (Rudolph)

I'm the guy who said, "Give me liberty or give me death!" (Patrick Henry)

I'm the guy who comes only once a year. (Santa Claus)

I'm the guy who said, "Arise, the British are coming." (Paul Revere)

I'm the guy who said, "Et tu, Brute." (Julius Caesar)

I'm the guy who said, "Four score and seven years ago." (Abraham Lincoln)

I'm the little island where they sing "Farewell to Thee." (Hawaii)

I'm the guy who flew the Atlantic alone. (Charles Lindbergh)

I'm the gal who was the Governor of Texas. (Ma Ferguson)

I'm the guy who fiddled while Rome burned. (Nero)

I'm the guy who said, "I do not choose to run." (Calvin Coolidge)

I'm the guy who worked fourteen years for the gal he loved. (Jacob)

I'm the guy who said, "To be or not to be, that is the question." (Hamlet)

I'm the guy who gave fireside chats. (Franklin D. Roosevelt)

I'm the guy who said, "Oh say, can you see . . ." (Francis Scott Key)

I'm the gal who was lost while flying in the South Pacific. (Amelia Earhart)

I'm the guy who loved Jonathan. (David)

I'm the gal who wore a glass slipper. (Cinderella)

I'm the gal famous for my "bangs." (Mamie Eisenhower)

I'm the guy who signaled V for victory. (Winston Churchill)

I'm the gal who saved France. (Joan of Arc)

I'm the gal who said, "Mary had a little lamb." (Mother Goose)

I'm the guy who says, "People are funny." (Art Linkletter)

— I'm the guy who is the Governor of (name your state).

— I'm the guy who is president of the organization giving the affair, or a leader of the organization who is present.

— I'm the gal who is the wife of a leader present.

— I'm the gal who cooked the banquet (or prepared refreshments, or is the leader of this game).

— We're the guys and gals who say, "Let's eat" (everyone will shout names or some word of agreement).

Variations:

It's fun to use the game as a contest between two sides. Appoint a leader for each team to help decide which side wins each point and to hold the candy until the game is completed. Players stand, teams facing each other with a line drawn between. As one person answers he steps across the line shouting the answer. If one side has the wrong answer, the opposing team gets the candy.

For older adults, put men in one team and women in the other. They can remain seated and raise hands.

It's fun to match girls with the boys in the contest groups. This is a game that can be used for almost any event.

(Used with permission of Cecile Steeds, Oklahoma City, Okla.)

24. Can You Do As I Do?

Materials:

Two hats (men's preferred), two chairs.

Formation:

Informal seated circle, players facing center of circle, or stage.

Directions:

Place two chairs, facing each other, about two feet apart on stage, or where everybody can see them. The leader takes part in this stunt until some player feels he can do the act. A volunteer from the group sits in the chair facing the leader. Holding the two hats, the leader asks the other person which hat he would like to wear. When the player has chosen a hat, the leader says he would like to tell a story. But, the guest must do the exactly opposite to anything the leader does as he tells the story. When the leader stands, the player sits; when the leader sits, the other stands. If the leader puts his hat on, the other takes his hat off, and so on. The leader keeps his story going as he sits, stands, takes the hat off, puts it on, until the guest fails to keep up with him or gets so confused he gives up. The player then appoints someone to take his place, or the leader may call for a volunteer. The leader may tell any sort of story, trying to get the guest so interested in the story that he forgets his actions. The leader should go through the actions rapidly, so as to help confuse the other player.

Variation:

Use at the close of an affair to honor the winners of contest games. Instead of telling a story, the leader can ask
questions about how they won the contest or other
questions about themselves to keep their attention from
the acting.

For a simple variation, or for use with young children,
use just the actions and omit the story.

25. The Last Shall Be First

Material:

A list of cities, or fruits, vegetables, or any other subject.

Formation:

Seated in a circle or around a table, with leader as head of circle.

Directions:

The leader calls the name of a city and starts counting. Before the leader can count to ten, the player on the leader's right must name a city that begins with the last letter of the city called. Example: leader calls "New Orleans," and the player to the right calls "Seattle." Each player must name a city before the leader counts ten. The one who fails to do so moves to the end which will be the immediate left of leader. All players move up. Leader should keep the game moving rapidly. The first-place winner is the one who can remain longest in the head chair.

Variation:

The leader can point to any player each time instead of going around the circle. He may have a chair by his side and calls a player to sit there. Then as he points to various players he quickly points to the one in the chair, trying to catch him off guard. If the player fails to answer he goes back to his vacant seat and another player is selected. The winner will be the one who can stay in the honor chair the longest.

This game can be used also at a Bon Voyage party or luncheon, using a list of things the traveler will see or might bring back as a gift.

26. Word Scouting

Materials:

Small white cards in small box. Write letters of alphabet on cards, one letter to a card. Place them in a box. If group is more than fifteen in number, provide at least four cards of each vowel and other letters used most often.

Formation:

Informal circle or around a table.

Directions:

Shuffle the cards face down so that group cannot see the letters. Pick a card, hold it up so that group can see the letter, and call out, "Name a bird." The first player to name a bird beginning with that letter gets the card. If no one answers in five seconds, return the card to the box and draw again.

Use such directions as "Name a girl"—or boy, car, car part, color, food, clothing, fruit, city, river, but give no clues as to the subject to be named each time. Subjects may be repeated, but the player may not repeat a name that has been given earlier. A large number of cards will be needed to keep the game going and to let everyone participate. The person holding the largest number of cards at the end of the game is the winner.

27. Rabbit, Man, Gun (a real brain teaser)

Material:

None.

Formation:

Select two captains and form parallel lines by numbering off, or use two words BING and BANG. Captain No. 1 will be BING, Captain No. 2 will be BANG. Bing will face Bang in receiving instructions.

Directions:

Leader explains and demonstrates the actions that represent the three characters, Rabbit, Man, and Gun. *Rabbit* is represented by poking thumbs in ears and waving fingers held tightly together as rabbit ears. *Man* is represented by standing very erect with arms down by sides. *Gun* is represented by pointing right index finger with thumb straight up and other fingers clenched in palm of hand to represent a shooting position.

At the signal each group goes into a huddle to decide which one of the three characters to represent. When the leader signals again, each side steps back into line facing each other. With everyone very quiet and waiting to perform, the leader counts 1, 2, 3. On the count of 3 each side steps forward about two steps closer to center, each person making the motion of the character his side has chosen.

How to Score

Man always wins over *Gun*, because Man can shoot with Gun.

Rabbit always wins over *Man*, because Rabbit can run faster than Man.

Gun always wins over *Rabbit,* because Gun can shoot Rabbit.

A team scores a point each time it outwits the other team. In case of a tie (such as Man against Man), no one scores.

When this game is played enthusiastically, it becomes a real test of wits to see which side can outguess the other. High school and college students have been known to play this game for an hour or more.

Variation:

For Thanksgiving, change *Rabbit* to *Turkey.* For Halloween, change *Man* to *Ghost.* For Valentine's Day, *Man* can be *Cupid, Rabbit* can become *Girl,* who is the weaker and runs from *Cupid,* and *Gun* can be *Arrow.*

28. Your Favorite Food

Material:

Prepare a list of foods ahead of time.

Formation:

Two teams facing each other, standing or across a table. Scorekeeper.

Directions:

Divide the group into two or more teams depending on the number of players. The leader calls the name of some item of food, such as "apple." Teams take turns in naming dish made with apples, such as apple pie, apple sauce. Team No. 1 begins the game. Team No. 2 starts off first when the second ingredient is named. The team that first runs out of words loses the point. Or the team that names the longest list of dishes for each ingredient can be declared the winner.

List of Ingredients

Banana	Cabbage	Buttermilk	Beans
Chocolate	Corn Meal	Carrots	Garlic
Eggs	Onion	Chicken	Cheese
Ground Beef	Potatoes, Irish	Fish	Rice

Variations:

For seasonal luncheons or dinners, prepare a list of objects and have each team alternate in naming what they would do with each object. Example, turkey: (1) kill it, (2) dress it, (3) bake it, (4) eat it, (5) fatten it, (6) sell its feathers, (7) make it gobble, and so on.

Suggested Objects

Poinsettia	Christmas stocking	Firecracker
Santa's reindeer	Christmas tree	Dinner plate
Doll	Valentine	Fork
Toy train	Heart candy	Napkin

(Idea taken from *Short Skits and Games for Women*. Zondervan Publishing House.)

29. Memory Exercise

Material:

List of names to be read. A judge to help check.

Formation:

Informal seating in circle or at tables, or as an audience.

Directions:

Announce that in order to test their memory for re-membering names, the group must repeat each name in unison. Each time a name is added, the group must repeat that name, go back to the first name called, and repeat each one in order, up to and including the last name. Example: the leader calls "John." The group re-peats "John." The leader calls "Sue." The group repeats "Sue, John, Sue," and so forth. This continues until at least ten names have been called, or as long as even one person repeats the names correctly. Each person who makes a mistake must drop out of the game. A list is suggested below. It can be more fun to make the list of those present, alternating man and woman.

List

Earl	Ruth	Agnes	Clara	Sara
Josephine	Henry	James	Keith	Charles
Edward	Louise	Irma	Rachael	Eva
Mary	John	Jay	Odell	Don

Variation:

Divide group into two teams with a captain for each. Draw straws for first go; each captain has his list and alternates in calling the names. The winner will be the team that can call back correctly the longest list.

(Idea of this game taken from *Short Skits and Games for Women*. Zondervan.)

30. This Is the Bunny

Material:

None.

Formation:

Seated facing leader at front.

Directions:

This amusing finger-play game is a restful game to play after an active one, or it can be used as a fill-in. Demonstrate the motions for the characters in the story. For *Rabbit,* each person puts his thumbs in his ears, with fingers waving back and forth for ears. For *Carrot,* place index fingers together pointing down. For *Hole in the Ground,* each player makes an O with thumb and index finger together. For *Might,* flex the arm muscles. *Noise* is represented by bringing hands up to ears. To "jump in the hole" each player pops four fingers of right hand into hole made by left hand. The leader should demonstrate the actions first. Then the story can be read slowly, until the group understands. It should be read rapidly and acted out several times.

Story

"This is the bunny,
With his ears so funny.
And this is the hole in the ground.
This is his carrot bright,
He eats with all his might.
But when a noise he hears,
He pricks up his ears—
And jumps in the hole in the ground."

(Used with permission of Harper and Row, New York)

31. Ten Little Squirrels

Material:

None.

Formation:

Seated or standing in a group facing leader.

Directions:

This finger-play game makes a restful activity or an easy fill-in.

Teach the motions before starting the story.

Story

Ten little squirrels (raise both hands, palms out and finger tips even with shoulders),
Up in a tree (raise hands up above head).
First little squirrel says (hold up index fingers),
"WHAT IS IT THAT I SEE?" (in excited voice here).
Second little squirrel says (hold up two fingers),
"OH, GEE! IT'S A MAN WITH A GUN." (Hold up thumbs and index fingers pointing, making a gun.)
Third little squirrel says (hold up three fingers),
"WOW, WOW, LET'S RUN." (Wiggle fingers as though running away.)
Fourth little squirrel says (four fingers),
"OH, NO, LET'S HIDE IN THE SHADE!" (Pull all fingers into a fist as though hiding.)
Fifth little squirrel says (holding up little fingers),
"AH, PSHAW! I'M NOT AFRAID!" (Leader stretches both arms out in position to pop the gun—waits until audience is in the same position. Leader draws a deep breath, then shouts:)
"POP GOES THE GUN!" (Clap hand loudly.)
"SEE THEM ALL RUN!" (Wiggle fingers, stretching hands wide apart again.)

Variation:

When using this game with youngsters, divide the group into five sections to represent the five squirrels and let each group act out its part, when the leader points to it. On the last line, all shoot the gun and run.

This type of finger-play can be developed to fit many situations. The plot is simple to adapt.

(Used with permission of Harper and Row, New York)

Chapter 4

INSTANT MUSICAL FUN

32. Old MacDonald Had a Farm

Material:

Provide music for pianist or use without piano.

Formation:

Either seated or standing.

Directions:

This is a variation of the well-known children's game. Leader explains the motions and drills the group by counting 1 -2 - 3 - 4. On count No. 1, clap hands in front of body at chest level; on count No. 2, while holding the nose with the right hand, grab the right ear with the left hand; on count No. 3, clap hands as before. On No. 4, hold nose with the left hand and grab left ear with right hand. Repeat counting on each action to catch rhythm until several players have caught the action. Then start the song. The hand clap is always count No. 1.

Words

Old MacDonald had a farm, E - I - E - I - O,
And on this farm he had some chicks, E - I - E - I - O,
With a chick chick here, and a chick chick there,
Here a chick, there a chick, everywhere a chick chick,
Old MacDonald had a farm, E - I - E - I - O.
(Repeat with as many verses as the group may wish to do.)

Other verses are:

Duck—(quack, quack)   Turkey—(gobble, gobble)
Pig—(oink, oink)   Well—(drip, drip)

Hay—(bail, bail)   Cat—(me-ow, me-ow)
Hoe—(chop, chop)   Wife—(giv'me, giv'me)

Variation:

Use as a stunt with six or eight people called out of audience to come to the front to perform.

33. Did You Ever

Materials:

Piano, and list of compound nouns. The ones listed are only a few of the many that can be included. Tune— "The More We Get Together."

Formation:

Seated, or standing in parallel lines or sections, or seated at various tables at a banquet or luncheon.

Directions:

Divide the guests into two or more groups, or use natural divisions if at separate tables. Each group or table should select its own song leader.

Toss a coin for first go. The first leader and his group sing a verse using a compound noun such as "horse fly."

Words (to the old tune)

Did you ever see a horse fly, a horse fly, a horse fly,
Did you ever see a horse fly, a horse fly, fly, fly, fly.
(Second group replies):
Did you ever see a board walk, a board walk, a board walk,
Did you ever see a board walk, a board walk, walk, walk, walk.

While one group is performing, the other groups are thinking of a response word. If one group cannot think of a response within ten seconds, another group can pick it up. This game is a good laugh maker, and can be used with almost any group.

Suggested List

cow slip
steeple chase
shoe lace
toe nail
hair pin
tooth pick
tongue lash
eye drop
neck tie
house fly

moth ball
nose drop
eye lash
tooth brush
butter fly
hand saw
ear drum
hair brush
wrist watch
yard stick

34. Li'l Liza Jane (action song)

Material:

Almost everyone knows the words, but they can be on a blackboard, if necessary.

Formation:

Seated, facing song leader.

Directions:

The song leader or different groups of players sing the verse, while everybody claps hands in rhythm. On the refrain, everybody jumps up, waves both hands high above head, sings in a pleading manner "O, Li'l Liza," and sits down on the word "Jane." Repeat these actions for every chorus.

Li'l Liza Jane

1. I got a gal an' you got none, Li'l Liza Jane,
   I got a gal an' you got none, Li'l Liza Jane.
   Refrain:
   O Li'l Liza, Li'l Liza Jane,
   O Li'l Liza, Li'l Liza Jane.

2. Come my love an' live with me, Li'l Liza Jane,
   I will take good care of thee, Li'l Liza Jane.
   Refrain: repeat

3. Got a house and lot in Baltimore, Li'l Liza Jane,
   Lots of chickens 'round the door, Li'l Liza Jane.
   Refrain: repeat

4. Every morning when you awake, Li'l Liza Jane,
   Smell the ham and buckwheat cake, Li'l Liza Jane.

35. My Bonnie Lies Over the Ocean

Material:

None.

Formation:

Seated, with ample space for movement of body when standing.

Directions:

Explain this action song by demonstrating it. Then let the audience run through it slowly once or twice. When everyone has caught on, sing it several times, going faster each time.

Words	*Motion*
My	Hands across the chest.
Bonnie	Hands outline the curves of a pretty girl.
lies	Lay head on both hands on left shoulder.
over	Both hands together throwing over right shoulder.
the ocean	Wave both hands from right to left at chest level to indicate water rippling over rocks.

My Bonnie lies over Repeat motions above, up to "sea."

the sea	Right hand shading eyes, looking out to *sea.* (turning head from right to left)

(Third phrase is repeat of first phrase.)

Oh	Make circle O with thumb and index finger, arm outstretched so all can see.
bring	Right hand beckoning her to come.

back	Bring right hand to slap back over shoulders.
my	Hands across chest.
Bonnie	Same motion—two little curves.
to me	Pointing to self.

Refrain: Repeat necessary action.

Variation:

Use this action song as entertainment by letting a small group sing it in front of an audience.

36. Musical Tumult

Materials:

Write titles of familiar songs on small strips of paper. Number depends on size of group. Paper and pins.

Formation:

Informal.

Directions:

The leader and a helper pin a song strip on the back of each guest. At a signal, the group mixes and each player begins singing the song he sees on the back of any other player, changing songs as he moves around. At the same time, each player tries to identify the song on his own back.

When he thinks he has discovered the title, he goes to the leader to confirm it. If correct, he steps out of the game; if incorrect, he continues his search. Each player tries to keep the other players from identifying their songs. The last to find out his own song must sing it as a solo. Use duplicates in the song list if the group is large. Play this game at least twice by collecting and redistributing the slips.

Variation:

Use four slips for each song, thus reducing the number of titles, and making them easier to detect. Then when each has discovered what his title is, place similar titles together, forming quartets. Each group in turn must present its song, possibly improvising costume and sets.

37. Table Rhythm

Material:

List of popular songs on a chalkboard or poster, or typed lists for the number of leaders needed.

Formation:

Seated at tables or divided into groups.

Directions:

Appoint a song leader for each table or group. Table 1 starts singing the first song on the list. It stops at any spot in the song and table 2 picks up with the next word where No. 1 stopped. If table 2 sings the song completely, then table 3 must start immediately on the second song on the list, following the same procedure with table 4, and so on. When the last table has had its turn, table 1 picks up in order. The song leader at each table can try to catch the other tables by surprise, or stop the song at a different spot.

Continue until the list of songs has been completed or until all tables have dropped out except one. If a table cannot pick up and complete a song in its turn, that table is eliminated.

Variations:

Adapt the songs to the occasion. For a seasonal party such as Christmas, use popular Christmas songs. For children, use Mother Goose Rhymes. For Valentine's Day, love songs. For patriotic occasions, patriotic songs. For birthdays, use songs with girls' names, or with boys' names. Lists can be prepared ahead of time.

38. The Broken Record

Material:

A large number of Mother Goose rhymes written on small cards.

Formation:

Informal circle after numbering off 1 - 2 - 1 - 2 for partners. Or use partners from a previous game.

Directions:

Select a couple at random to stand up facing the group. Give the couple one of the cards with a rhyme. At the signal, the couple starts reading dramatically in unison. At another signal, the couple must repeat the word they were saying until cut off by the leader. The object is to see how many couples can sound like a broken record perfectly on the first try.

Variation:

Type a number of popular songs for each couple to sing. They should continue the song until it is recognizable before the signal stops them, and sends them into the broken record repetition.

INSTANT FUN

WITH SKITS
AND STUNTS

Chapter 5

THE MATERIAL in this section requires practically no preparation or rehearsal on the part of the audience or group. The leader, of course, has to be thoroughly familiar with it.

The skits and stunts fall primarily into two types. The first type includes stunts in which some individual or group is led into a surprising and sometimes absurd situation or practical joke. Stunt No. 41 is typical of Type I.

Type II consists mostly of stunts and skits based on a story or other narrative told or recited by the leader while the audience or group participates by pantomime, oral response, or other action. These are sometimes called audience-response stunts. They are interesting to all age groups and make excellent icebreakers.

A word of warning about Type I: be *very* sure of the person or group before putting anyone into a ridiculous situation, or making him the butt of a practical joke. Use such material sparingly. Hurt feelings or embarrassment on anyone's part can spoil any activity or event.

39. The Mexican Prisoner

Materials:
About 25 matches and a table.

Formation:
This is a good stunt for small groups. For a large party, divide into smaller groups, and play the stunt at each table.

Directions:
The leader, holding the matches, tells the story. "In a recent Mexican conflict, a well-known guerilla was captured by his enemies and became known as the Mexican Prisoner. Here he is." (Leader puts a match on the table to represent the prisoner.)

"Because of his valor, the prisoner was feared and his captors decided to put him in a strong, square building in a lonely spot. Here is the building." (Place four matches around the prisoner for the building.)

"His captors so feared that he would escape, that they decided to place a special guard at each outer corner of the building. In this way, each wall could be under constant guard." (Leader places a match at each corner of the building.)

"These men were never to leave their post. It was arranged that each day their wives should bring them food. Here are the wives." (Place a match by the side of each guard.)

"The arduous nature of their watch, the fear of the Mexican Prisoner, the mountain air, the loneliness, all helped to make the guards eager for their food, and anxious that their wives should stay a while and eat with them. Thus it happened that the wives found they could not carry all the provisions required. They placed the food and drink on the backs of four donkeys. Here are the four donkeys."

(Place matches beside three of the wives, as if absent-mindedly failing to notice that the fourth was omitted. Go on with the story, recapitulating so that time is allowed for someone to fall into the trap.) "So you see we have the Mexican, and here are the four walls of his prison." (Points to the matches.) "Here are the four guards; and here are the four wives. . . ."

(By this time, if not long before, some eager person will correct the leader with the query), "But where is the fourth donkey?" (Leader quickly replies), "Well, my dear, I left that place vacant especially for you."

40. And the Waves Beat upon the Rocks

Formation:

Leader places characters in the playing space as story develops.

Directions:

Announce, "We have decided to put on a one-act play. Since we don't have time for a rehearsal of this play or to collect stage properties, we shall need some of you to run through the play quickly, and to set the scenes. For instance, we need two trees." (Select two men, stand one to the left and one center right. Place them with arms lifted and hands dangling to indicate branches. They should be at least six feet apart.)

"Now we need a beautiful moon." (Select a red-haired or blond woman, stationing her between the trees, directing her to smile brightly and broadly.

"How unromantic would an evening be, even with moon and trees, without gentle breezes to blow among the trees." Select two of the largest men in group, and show them how to trip around the trees, puffing and blowing, while the leaves of the trees wave and swing.

"Now, with a moon shining brightly, trees waving gently (in reality very vigorously), and breezes softly blowing (loud puffing and blowing), we must have a boat." Four people are selected to represent a boat. Those at each end rock their bodies to and fro, and those at each side sway their bodies from side to side.

"This is the perfect setting for two romantic lovers." Select a woman and a man to play the lovers, and seat them on chairs placed within the boat space.

"The scenery for this romantic occasion would not be complete, even with the beautiful moon shining brightly, the trees waving gently, and the breezes blowing softly, without rocks on the shore." Select five or six men—good sports who can take a joke—to kneel in a semicircle in front of the boat.

"Even with the moon beaming brightly, the trees waving gently, and breezes blowing softly, and the rocks adding their charm to the scene, we must have some waves to rock the boat for the lovers." Select women who have been briefed in advance—one wave for each rock—and give each a concealed paper swatter.

"We are now ready for the drama to begin: Once upon a time there were two lovers (lovers hold hands) who went for a boat ride on a beautiful night when the moon was shining brightly (moon beams broadly); the trees were swaying gently (trees sway vigorously); the breezes were blowing softly (puffing and blowing loudly); the boat was rocking lazily; and *"the waves were beating upon the rocks."* (At that moment, the women with the concealed swatters begin lashing the rocks. They continue until the rocks get the point and remove themselves from the situation. It sometimes lends more humor when the waves are the wives or dates of the rocks.)

Note: This stunt may be adapted to any number of participants, by using more players for breezes, trees, rocks, and so on.

41. Dental Impression

Material:

Paper napkins.

Formation:

Informal seating.

Directions:

As refreshments are being served, or after dessert has been finished at a luncheon, distribute a fresh paper napkin to each guest. Invite all guests to imitate your actions. Hold your napkin several different ways, open it out, twist it in the center, spread out the ends in the shape of a bow, take it in the center and hold it between your upper lip and nose as a mustache. Smile and nod your head as though making a speech, or singing. Then suddenly stick the middle part of the napkin in your mouth. When everyone has done the same, announce with a grin, "My, all of you do bite well."

42. The Lion and the Lamb

Material:

A copy of the story, if not memorized.

Formation:

Leader seated at piano.

Directions:

This is an entertainment stunt. The leader or the entertainer takes seat at piano, with the gestures of a real musician. He tells this story as if he were singing, and the piano interprets the action.

"Once there was a great, wide desert (strike the lowest and highest notes to show vast distance of desert).

"In the center of this torrid and withering desert, there were three, yes, three tiny trees (strike middle C E G slowly, one after the other).

"And, near these three little trees there was a refreshing, bubbling spring (play C D E D C one octave higher —play repeatedly a few times to represent bubbling water).

"One day a little lamb came trotting to the spring for a cool drink (slide with thumb rapidly from highest note to middle C).

"About that time a lazy mountain lion spied the situation and came trotting down to drink at the spring (slide somewhat more slowly from the lowest note to middle C).

"As the lazy mountain lion reached the spring and looked the situation over (run C E G from lowest to highest key slowly—then play the notes faster and faster).

"At that moment there was a great tragic commotion (with both hands strike all over keyboard to signify the commotion).

"Following this tragic commotion, the little lamb went home with the lion (slide slowly from middle C to highest note and from middle C to lowest note).

"Upon reaching the mountain lion's home, both sat down to rest (from middle C to play C E G with both hands rather slowly then sound complete chord for sitting).

"Soon the pangs of hunger began to rumble within the lion (make rumbling noise on piano lower keys).

"He arose to his feet and looked the situation over (make same note as when he was at the spring).

"He shook his shaggy tail (rumble lower keys again),

"And *pounced* on the wee little lamb (with both hands pounce all over the keyboard).

"Soon there was nothing left but three small trees (same sound as first for the trees),

"And a little bubbling spring (same as before—very dramatically),

"And a big lonely desert (same as before—slowly and dramatically).

"And a *lion full of lamb chops* (with both hands run up and down the keyboard—then make one big splash in the middle).

Variation:

One person can tell the story while another person plays the piano. Or guests can read the story in unison, with piano accompanist.

43. The Cat's Whiskers

Materials:

Broom straws, masking tape, a watch or a chain, or a small rubber or glass ball to use to hypnotize the player, a chair, and a rubber rat or mouse.

Formation:

Informal.

Directions:

Leader explains the basis of hypnosis and its power. A volunteer (who is in cahoots with the leader and who has the rubber rat already hidden in his pocket) offers to be the victim. The leader suggests that the volunteer can be made to think he is a cat, and they agree to try.

The leader swings the watch or chain or ball before the eyes of victim, waves hand over eyes, mumbling in a monotone until the victim slumps, eyes closed as if in sleep.

The leader announces that the subject is under hypnosis. He tapes straws on each cheek of the victim to make cat whiskers.

The cat then begins to stir, rubs his whiskers, licks his lips and paws, doing this in slow pantomime so that the audience can see. The leader then waves his hand in front of the cat's face, calls his name loudly. The cat jumps to his feet, gazes about, rubs his eyes, then storms out, "Why did you change me? I *liked* being a cat! I was so hungry I was ready to eat my dinner, and you changed me back."

He pulls the big rubber rat from his pocket saying, "Oh, what a wonderful dinner I was about to have! Now I'll give it to you for *your* dinner"—and he tosses the rat out to the women in the audience.

44. Little Red Riding Hood

Material:

If used for audience entertainment, prepare one sign with "Little Red Riding Hood" printed on it, to be held up when audience recognizes the story. The poem can be spoken by the leader alone; or, as he tells the story, two persons dressed to represent the Wolf and Little Red Riding Hood can act out the story as it is told.

Formation:

Informal seating.

Directions:

Leader introduces the drama or story, setting the stage for a much loved story of childhood. This script has been used very successfully with groups from eight to eighty years old. Energetic actors may memorize, but it should be done dramatically.

Little Red Riding Hood

Long years ago, as I've been told,
The animals were all very wise and bold;
They could act and talk like you and me,
And were just as cunning as cunning could be.

They roamed in the fields and the forests too,
And having nothing much else to do
They bothered people no little bit
By their mischievous manners and nimble wit.

The most of them were very kind
But every now and then one would find
A fox or a badger, wolf or bear
Who was quite a rascal and did not care.

There lived, they say, in that part of the world
A family who had only one little girl;
(They lived at the edge of a very great wood)
And her name was little (reader pauses here to let the
audience guess—all will shout out) "Little Red Riding
Hood."

One day her mother asked her to take
A basket filled with bread and some cake
To her dear grandmother who was very ill
And lived in a house just over the hill.

The little girl, feeling no sense of alarm,
Swung the basket over her arm
And started happily through the wood
To cheer her grandmother all she could.

She had not gone far until who should meet her
But old Mr. Wolf who stopped to greet her.
She knew of his very bad reputation,
So she spoke to him with great hesitation.

"Good morning, fair neighbor, and how do you do?
"May I have the pleasure of walking with you?
"The basket you carry must be quite a load;
"I'll carry it for you as we go down the road."

"I'm quite well, indeed, Sir; and pray how are you?"
She said quite politely, as children should do;
She felt such alarm that she barely could mask it,
As she timidly handed the old wolf her basket.

"Pray, where are you going this very fine day?
I'm happy indeed to be going your way."
The old wolf was thinking how fine it would be
To have Little Red Riding Hood for his tea.

"I'm going to Grandma's; she's been very sick."
The old wolf thought up a plan very quick—
"Oh, yes, my dear child," he said, nodding his head.
"You stay right on this road; I'll take this one instead."

"If she's needing a doctor, I'll rush into town
"And get one," he said, dashing off with a bound.
In less than a minute he was clear out of sight,
And he ate Grandma's bread and cake up in one bite.

Poor Grandma was lying quite still in her bed
When "knock, knock," she heard; "Who is it?" she said;
The wolf made his voice sound ever so mild
So Grandma would think he was her grandchild.

"It's I, dear Grandmother," he said, pulling the string,
Then entered the room all ready to spring.
He frightened poor Grandma almost to death,
And he swallowed her up before she could get a full
breath.

"My prize is most won," he said with a grin,
"For Red Riding Hood will be soon coming in."
He then dressed himself just like Grandmother
And jumped into bed and pulled up the cover.

Red Riding Hood knocked at her grandmother's door
Just as she often had knocked before,
Expecting her dear grandmother to greet her,
Not knowing the wolf had already "eat" her.

"It's I, Grandmother! May I come in?"
"Oh, yes dear," he said, with a voice very thin.
She lifted the latch and came inside—
When she saw her Grandma, her eyes got so wide!

"Oh, Grandmother, your eyes look so fierce and so wild!"
"The better to see you with, my child!"
"And Grandmother, how long your ears do appear!"
"The better to hear you with, my dear!"

"And what big teeth you have, Grandmother!"
"The better to eat you with, my daughter!"
The wicked wolf turned and jumped out of bed
And grabbed Red Riding Hood by the head;

And started to eat her in just one bite,
When the door swung open with all its might.
The woodmen had heard the child's awful wail—
They cut the old wolf from head to his tail.

He had swallowed old Grandmother whole, you remember,
And she sprang forth as bright as a night in December!
So this story ends as all good stories should—
Happily, for dear Little Red Riding Hood!

* * *

For less formal presentation, no costuming or set is required. Narrator reads or tells the story, and sections of the audience respond.

(Poem used by permission of author, Virginia Ely)

45. The Three Little Pigs

Materials:

Grandmother costume, makeup, rocking chair for the narrator. Sound effects for wolf-howl, pig-squeals, and wind-blowing. Small chairs for children to sit at knee of grandmother. Good story reader. For less formal presentation, no costuming or set is required.

Formation:

Informal seating, facing stage.

Directions:

Leader introduces play, and explains that at her signal, audience must squeal like pigs, howl like wolves, or puff like the wind. If dramatized, the pantomimes of grandmother and reader should be rehearsed. The story can be read without a grandmother or children pantomime.

The Three Little Pigs

Come, little children, and I shall tell
A story I think you will like very well.
It's about an old sow and three little pigs.
The mother was old. She had to wear wigs
And false teeth, and walk on a crutch,
And her eyes were so dim she couldn't see much.

One day when they were having their tea
She gathered her piggies close up to her knee
(*children move close in*)
And said: "My children, the time has now come
When each of you should have your own home;
I'm getting old, and I'll never die happy
If I fear you may go the same way as your pappy.

"We were living that spring near a beautiful pool,
Where the moss was so soft and the mud was so cool.
We had noticed at times a very strange track—
Your father followed it one day, and he never came
    back!
He followed the track almost to the door
Of the Big Bad Wolf *(wolf howls)*, and I saw him no
    more."

"When I heard the sad news, without waiting a minute,
I built me a house, and quickly moved in it;
For the neighbors had told me of Mr. Wolf's boast
Of dining each day on a juicy pork roast.
In a house of your own there is nothing to harm you,
So please do not let this story alarm you."

The first little piggy looked around *(pig squeal)* 'til he
    saw
A man who was hauling a big load of straw.
"Say, Mister!" *(squeals in squeaky voice)* he called in a
    thin little tone,
"Will you give me some straw to build me a home?"
He built his straw house by the side of the bog.
How foolish! but he was a foolish young hog.

He was no sooner in and turned on the lock,
When he heard the old wolf *(howls)* and his knock,
    knock, knock!
"Who's there," called the piggy, his face in a grin;
"It's I," said the wolf: "Won't you let me come in?"
"No! not by the hair of your chinny, chin, chin!"
"Then I'll blow and I'll blow 'til I blow your house in!"
(wind sound effects)
The wolf took one puff that was not very big,
But he blew down the house, and he ate up the pig.
    (slow squeal)

Then he waited nearby and watched the old mother,
As she bade fond adieu to the first piggy's brother.
The wolf planned to catch him just outside the gate,
But not being hungry he thought he would wait.

The piggy came out and he stood and he stood,
'Till he saw a man with a big load of wood;
Then he called to the man in a very fine tone:
"Mister, please give me some wood to build me a home."
He built him a house and had just turned the lock
When he heard the old wolf with his "knock, knock,
    knock!"

"Who's there?" called the piggy his face in a grin;
"It's I," said the wolf, "won't you let me come in?"
"No, not by the hair of your chinny, chin, chin!
"Then I'll blow and I'll blow 'til I blow your house in!"
    (*strong wind sounds*)
"Blow on, Mr. Wolf (*reader shouts*), with all of your
    might;
"Here's a piggy you won't get to eat with one bite!"

"Puff, Puff!" went the wolf, then how he did frown,
When the house stood staunch and did not tumble down.
He drew in his breath, it seemed almost an hour,
Then he turned it all loose with extremely great power:
"Plunk! Plunk!" came the house, then what a fine meal!
For the wolf ate all of the pig but his squeal.

The third little piggy was careful and quick.
He found him a man with a big load of brick.
"Mister," he called in a very brave tone,
"Will you give me some brick to build me a home?"
He finished his house and had just turned the lock,
When he heard the old wolf with his "knock, knock,
    knock!"

"Who's there?" called the piggy, his face in a grin.
"It's I," said the wolf, "won't you let me come in?"
"No, not by the hair of your chinny, chin, chin!"
"Then I'll blow, and I'll blow 'til I blow your house in!"
This caused the piggy to worry and bother,
For, of course, he remembered the fate of his father.

The old wolf puffed both loud and long,
But still the house stood staunch and strong;
He said: "Such nonsense makes me sick.
Just think of a pig in a house of brick!
He certainly is trying to put on style,
But I'll teach him something in a little while."
   (very dramatic reading)

"Dear Piggy," he said, "Can't we be friends?
I'm sorry and I want to make amends
For the way I've acted. If you'll forgive,
In peace and harmony we can live."
The piggy grunted *(sounds):* "He's full of jokes;
Does he think I'll swallow his clever hoax?"

The old wolf continued: "I understand
Some fine greens are growing on the land
That is owned by the Farmer in the Dell;
I've been there before and I know the place well.
If you'll go with me, we'll set a date,
And get off some morning before it gets late."

"Tomorrow will suit me," the piggy replied;
"I'm happy that I shall have you for my guide.
I think we should start no later than six."
(The piggy was also full of his tricks)
The old wolf thought: "How clever I am!
Tomorrow I'll feast on a nice piece of ham."

The piggy got up on the last stroke of four.
By six he was already back at his door,
And watching with quite a mischievous eye
To see the wolf when he came trotting by;
He shut up the house 'til he thought he would smother,
Because he recalled the advice of his mother.

"I'm sorry," he said, when the wolf came along;
"I waited for you, but my clock was all wrong.
And I have already been to the patch,
And gathered my greens," he said, turning the latch.
To tell such a story he knew was a sin,
But he also knew the wolf wanted his skin.

The wolf was as mad as a wolf could well be,
But he said: "I know of a very sweet apple tree
Where apples are hanging, red, juicy, and big."
(He knew the best method of tempting a pig.)
"Let's pay them a visit tomorrow at five."
"By six," he thought, "Mr. Pig won't be alive."

"All right," said the piggy, looking quite wise;
("I'll be back by five; that will be his surprise.
I would not go with him for all the world's wealth
Because it would be very bad for my health.")
He got up next morning promptly at four,
And thought he would work the same trick as before.
He had taken his perch on a very high limb,
(Not knowing the wolf stood looking at him)
And had eaten and eaten 'til he had his fill,
When he saw Mr. Wolf at the foot of the hill.
"O mercy! O me! Now what shall I do!"
The sight of the wolf scared him through and through.

"Hey, Piggy, throw me an apple," he said.
The old wolf had laughed 'til his face had turned red.

For he thought, "I have him right now in my hands;
This works out far better than even I planned;
He thought it was funny to run off from me,
And now he is out on the limb of a tree."

The pig threw the apple; it rolled down the hill;
The wolf chased the apple and chased it until
The piggy had time to get down from the limb
And run home before the wolf could catch him.
The wolf had one more trick up his sleeve
Which he feared the piggy would hardly believe.

He said, when he came to the house in a huff:
"Mr. Piggy, this thing has gone far enough;
Such rough stuff isn't funny to me,
But you like it full well, it's quite plain to see.
However, to show you I'm not of that ilk
I'll lead you to some very fine buttermilk."

They both planned to start the next morning at four;
The pig got up early, as he had twice before.
He said, "I'll take my ten-gallon churn,
And bring home enough buttermilk to burn."
He had started back home in a very high spirit;
When he got to the gate, the wolf was right near it!
    (a tense moment, very dramatic)

The pig saw the wolf and the wolf saw the pig,
And both of their hearts went jiggity-jig;
The wolf stretched himself out so he could run,
The piggy said: "Oh, if I just had a gun!"
Poor piggy! he didn't know which way to turn,
So he poured out the milk and jumped in the churn.

The churn started rolling. It rolled very fast.
The pig did not know that the wolf had been passed.

He had no idea he was even close to his door
'Till he crashed it wide open and rolled out on the floor.
He had twisted and turned, 'til no word he could utter,
For he had pounded and churned like a mold of fresh
　butter.

The pig shut the door and had turned on the lock,
When he heard Mr. Wolf with his "knock, knock,
　knock!"
The wolf started climbing all over the house;
(The piggy sat still as a scared little mouse)
When he got to the chimney, his eyes opened wide—
"Now I see a way I'll get inside."

Piggy swung in the fireplace a big dinner pot,
And filled it with water that soon was real hot;
He heard the wolf coming—he fell in, "ker-splash!"
The lid was capped on as quick as a flash;
And the third little piggy, you see, was the winner,
For that night he had boiled wolf for his dinner!

(Poem used by permission of author, Virginia Ely)

46. The Three Bears (a puppet show)

Materials:

Puppets to represent Goldilocks and each of the three bears, puppet stage, props, children or adults to operate the puppets, and a reader.

This skit can be played like "The Three Little Pigs," without puppets or other dramatization.

Formation:

Informal seating, facing stage.

Directions:

If puppets are used, the skit requires rehearsal. Otherwise the narrator introduces the story, and asks the audience to whistle when Goldilocks is mentioned, and to growl when the three bears speak—deeply for Papa Bear, middle-size growl for Mama Bear, and a little growl for Baby Bear.

The Three Bears

This story that I shall tell to you
Is not very old and not very new;
It's about a little blond girl
Who lived on the other side of the world.

She was not very bad and not very good,
And lived with her parents in a great big wood.
She had many toys and pretty frocks,
And her name was little Goldilocks.

One day when she was out at play
She decided that she would run away
And see what she could find in the world—
Such a naughty act for a little girl!

She ran and ran 'til she came to a house
And creeping up as still as a mouse
She quietly opened the big front door
And peeped in once, and then once more.

"I'll knock," she said, "upon the door;
If no one answers, I'll then explore
This little house that looks so queer
You'd hardly think that folks live here."

She knocked and knocked with all her might;
She looked to the left and then to the right;
Then feeling sure that no one was there
She entered the home of a *Big Brown Bear!*

The bear, as I often have been told
Had taken his family out for a stroll.
His family was really very small—
Just a wife and a baby, and that was all.

The baby was big enough to walk
And he could feed himself and talk.
The mama was called "The Middle-Size Bear,"
And she gave the baby lots of care.

They had made some soup of a juicy hare—
A very great delicacy for a bear,
And thought they would wait by the lily pool
And give the soup some time to cool.

Goldilocks opened her eyes very wide—
The soup was the first thing that she spied:
"I'll taste this soup in the great big bowl."
But she did not like it—it was too cold.

"This seems to be for a smaller tot."
She did not like that; it was too hot.
The soup was just right in the Little Bear's bowl,
And she tasted it all, so I am told.

She thought she would like to sit down and rest,
And decided to see which chair was the best—
She sat down first in the great big chair,
But it was too hard—it was made for a bear.

The middle-size chair was the next she tried,
But it was too soft—it was made of deer hide.
The Little Bear's chair was just right, no doubt,
For she sat 'til she sat the bottom out.

Then not dreaming that she was in the home of bears
She decided to look around upstairs
Three snowy-white beds stood side by side.
The Big Bear's bed was the first she tried.

"This bed is too hard," she said;
"I think I'll try the middle-size bed."
"And this one's too soft, I just declare."
So she crawled in the bed of the Little Bear.

Without even having to count any sheep
Goldilocks soon fell fast asleep.
The bears came back from the lily pool
When they thought the soup had had time to cool.

They came in through the big front door
Just as they always had before.
The Big Bear stopped with a snort and a sneer
And said, "Mrs. Bruin, someone's been here!"

"I know by that strange scent I smell—
"If I find him he won't fare so well."
The Middle-Size Bear was filled with fright;
She picked up the baby and held him tight.

"Now Cubby, don't you make a sound,
"And I'll begin to look around,"
Said the great Big Bear, looking very grim,
And the others followed after him.

"Somebody's been tasting my soup," said the father;
"Somebody's been tasting *my* soup," said the mother;
"Somebody's been tasting *my* soup," said the baby,
"And tasted it all, and I don't mean maybe!"

"Somebody's been sitting in my big chair,"
"And in mine, too," sniffed the Middle-Size Bear;
Big tears came to the Little Bear's eyes
As he looked at his chair in great surprise.

"Somebody sat in *my* chair, too,
"And sat the bottom out, boo, hoo!"
There never were three more angry bears
As hand in hand they went upstairs.

"Somebody's been sleeping in my big bed,"
"And in mine too," the mother said.
The Little Bear only gave a peep
At the little girl who was fast asleep.

The yell he gave would disturb the dead,
And Goldilocks jumped right out of bed
And ran as fast as ever she could,
'Til she came to her own house in the great big wood.

Variation:

Use as a pantomime, with players in costume. Beds
can be improvised by using benches with bed cover-
ing. Younger boys and girls enjoy dramatizing the story.

(Poem used by permission of author, Virginia Ely)

Chapter 6

INSTANT FUN

WITH RIDDLES

EVERYBODY ENJOYS RIDDLES, and so they are excellent ice-breakers and handy in-between fillers. You will think of many more riddles that you can add to these forty.

47. Forty Riddles to Guess

Material:

None.

Formation:

Informal.

Directions:

Use as fill-in between acts, games announcements, introductions, or other occasions when an icebreaker is needed.

When is a ship under water? . . . When it is on fire.

What is the best way to make a coat last? . . . Make vest and trousers first.

What is it that belongs to you entirely, and yet is used more by your friends than by yourself? . . . Your name.

What is the difference between a millionaire and a prize fighter? . . . One makes money hand over fist, and the other makes his fist hand over money.

Why is "B" like a fire? . . . Because it makes oil boil.

If a man gave one son 15 cents and another 10 cents, what time would it be? . . . A quarter to two.

Which is worth more, an old five-dollar bill or a new one? . . . An old five, because it is worth four dollars more.

Why is an old riddle like a broken pencil? . . . Because it has no point.

What makes time fly? . . . So many people trying to kill it.

What vowel has the jolliest time? . . . U because it is always in the middle of FUN.

Where was Solomon's temple? . . . On the side of his forehead.

Why must a physician keep his temper? . . . Because if he doesn't, he will lose his patience (patients).

Why is a coal stove like an artist? . . . Because it is no good unless it draws.

Under what circumstances is it all right to lie? . . . When in bed.

What is the hardest key to turn? . . . The donkey.

Why do sailors always wear white hats? . . . To cover their heads.

What is it that always runs, but never gets anywhere? . . . A clock.

Why is a washwoman the greatest traveler in the world? . . . Because she crosses the lines and goes from pole to pole.

When is a sheep like ink? . . . When you put it in a pen.

When is the worst weather for rats and mice? . . . When it rains cats and dogs.

What is always behind time? . . . The back of a watch.

Why is a dog's tail like the heart of a tree? . . . Because it is the farthest away from the bark.

Which is the swiftest, heat or cold? . . . Heat, because you can catch cold.

What is the difference between an engineer and a teacher? . . . One minds the train and the other trains the mind.

When is a door not a door? . . . When it's ajar.

What has teeth but never eats? . . . A comb.

How does a leopard change his spots? . . . When he moves from place to place.

What letter of the alphabet is necessary to a shoemaker? . . . "Z" because it's the last.

What is a put-up job? . . . Paper on the wall.

Why does the gatekeeper punch a hole in your ticket? . . . To let you through.

What does everybody in the world do at the same time? . . . Grow older.

When is water like a lion? . . . When it makes a spring.

Why is the letter "K" one of the most fortunate letters in the alphabet? . . . Because it is always in LUCK.

How do bees dispose of their honey? . . . They cell (sell) it.

If a farmer can raise 250 bushels of grain in dry weather, what can he raise in wet weather? . . . An umbrella.

What is it that you can keep even after giving it to someone else? . . . Your word.

At what time of day was Adam created? . . . A little before Eve.

What is the difference between a fisherman and a lazy schoolboy? . . . One baits the hook and the other hates the book.

Why is a buckwheat cake like a caterpillar? . . . Because it's the grub that makes the butterfly.

What is the difference between a hill and a pill? . . . One is hard to get up and the other hard to get down.